3.75

STARTING WITH
Stained Glass

By PAUL W. WOOD

**LITTLE
CRAFT BOOK
SERIES**

STERLING
PUBLISHING CO., Inc.   New York
SAUNDERS OF TORONTO, Ltd., Don Mills, Canada

Oak Tree Press Co., Ltd.
London & Sydney

Little Craft Book Series

Dedicated to my wife Jacqueline and our four sons.

The author wishes especially to thank Mr. Burton Hobson for his advice in the original planning of this book and his assistance in the preparation of the text and layout.

Thanks are also due my son Paul who helped with the photography and who demonstrated the various techniques in the step-by-step procedures.

Fourth Printing, 1977

Copyright © 1973 by Sterling Publishing Co., Inc.
Two Park Avenue, New York, N.Y. 10016
Distributed in Australia and New Zealand by Oak Tree Press Co., Ltd.,
P.O. Box J34, Brickfield Hill, Sydney 2000, N.S.W.
Distributed in the United Kingdom and elsewhere in the British Commonwealth
by Ward Lock Ltd., 116 Baker Street, London W 1

Contents

Before You Begin

New techniques and modern materials make it possible for the craftsman to use traditional stained glass in fresh, creative ways. Originally used primarily for religious windows, stained glass now brings color and light to homes and commercial buildings.

Here in simple, easy-to-follow steps is everything you need to know to work with this jewel-like transparent material. Beginning with an attractive hanging ornament, you are introduced directly to the techniques of the craft. The progressively more difficult projects that follow give you a chance to develop your skill and exercise your own creativity.

Materials

Some pieces of stained glass are, of course, the first requirement. If you are near a commercial stained glass workshop, you can probably purchase scrap glass of various types, colors, and textures from them. Many shops also offer small quantities of lead, solder, and other essentials to individual craftsmen. More and more art and craft supply shops are carrying stock of stained glass materials and, in the larger cities, professional stained glass supply houses will handle large orders.

Some craftsmen look for odd pieces of colored glass along the beach or in old trash heaps. You can often fit a piece of an old broken bottle of an interesting color into a project. Louis Tiffany, famous for his lamps, often used pieces of broken bottles, first melting them together in a kiln, to produce his special variegated glass.

Tools

In addition to a few common household tools, you will need only a mat knife or a linoleum knife for cutting the lead came, a glass cutter, a soldering iron and a pair of needle-nosed pliers.

Glass cutters have a small wheel at the tip that does the actual scoring. The different-sized notches are used to break off thin strips or rough pieces of glass.

Stained Glass Hanging Ornament

Materials Checklist:
- Small pieces of stained glass
- Glass cutter
- Mat knife
- Needle-nosed pliers
- Soldering iron
- Solder with flux core
- $\frac{1}{8}''$ U-shaped lead came
- Steel wool

Designs based on birds, flowers, fruits, or insects are especially suitable for stained glass hanging ornaments. Choose a subject that interests you and, keeping the shapes simple since these are easier to cut, draw a full-size design. Use soft charcoal or black felt-tip marker. The outline design must be dark enough to show through the colored glass which you will be cutting directly over the pattern. Select the stained glass for your ornament by holding pieces of various colors up to the window to see their appearance with light coming through. This will show you the true color effect which is often quite different than it seems when viewed against a solid surface.

You can make all sorts of decorative designs into patterns for hanging ornaments or free-standing forms mounted on a solid base.

With simple shapes, you can score the glass piece directly over the pattern. Sharp, difficult curves require preliminary scoring and breaking to work up to the final cut.

Cutting Glass

To cut glass, you first score it with a cutter and then break it along the scored line. To begin, lay a piece of colored glass over the pattern for the largest shape of that color. Try to utilize the existing edges of the glass whenever possible. Score the glass, following the pattern underneath. Hold the cutter with the wheel pressed downwards against the glass with the notched edge of the cutter towards you. The ball end of the cutter goes between your first two fingers: your thumb and index finger should be in position to bear down on the shoulders of the cutter. Dipping the wheel in kerosene or turpentine occasionally will lubricate it, making your job easier. Be sure to place the pattern and glass on a sturdy, flat surface.

Bearing down firmly with the cutter wheel, start at the edge away from you and draw the cutter steadily towards you. Maintain the downward pressure all the way to the other edge. Bear down hard enough so that the scoring shows clearly on the glass. Remember, though, you are only scoring the glass, not trying to cut all the way through it!

After the glass has been scored, you are ready to break it. If you are breaking the glass along a straight line, and if you have enough glass to hold it firmly on both sides of the line, press the pattern piece flat against the table with one hand so that the scored line is just along or slightly beyond the edge of the table. Grasp the excess glass firmly with your other hand and snap downward. The glass will break off along the scored line.

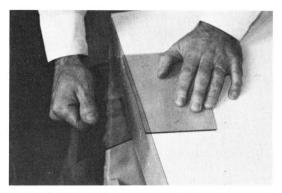

If the glass piece is large enough for you to grasp it on both sides of the scored line, place the piece so that the scored line is slightly beyond and parallel to the edge of the work table. Snap downward and the glass will break off along the scored line. To cut off a narrow piece, tap along under the scored line with the ball of the cutter.

To cut off pieces less than one inch wide, score the glass as above but break it off by tapping from below with the cutter along the length of the scored line. Curved cuts are scored in the same manner and also broken by tapping. Cut off very narrow pieces by scoring the glass, and then break off the excess using one of the notches on the side of the glass cutter. Uneven protrusions of glass along the cut edge can be smoothed off by working away at them with the notched teeth of the cutter (this is called "grozing").

With a reasonable amount of care, you can handle, cut, and assemble stained glass with little danger of cutting yourself. Sensible precautions, however, help prevent accidents. Do not put away glass with sharp projections pointing outwards. Professional stained glass craftsmen dull the edges by scraping the edge of a piece of scrap glass along them. Have a scrap box handy for the disposal of small pieces while you are cutting.

To break off very thin pieces of glass or any uneven protrusions, use the teeth of the glass cutter. Use the notch nearest in size to the thickness of the glass itself.

7

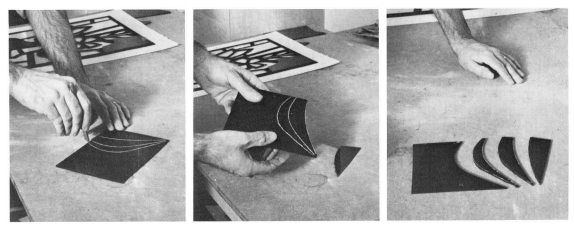

To cut a deep curve, first score two more gradual curves next to it. Use your glass cutter to tap out the first piece of glass, then the second and the third. Any curve sharper than this requires two pieces of glass joined by a lead at the sharpest part of the curve.

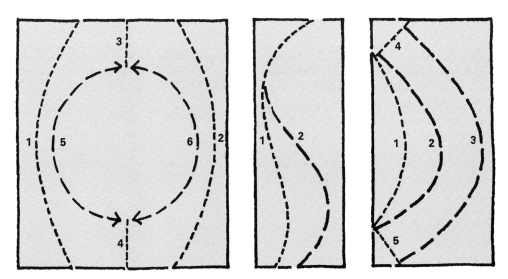

For cutting difficult shapes such as circles, S-shaped or elbow curves, several cuts are needed as indicated above.

When you have all of the pieces of glass for your ornament carefully cut to pattern, use transparent tape to attach them to a pane of clean clear glass and hold it against the light for a final color check before you start leading.

Kinds of Lead Came

1. Standard H-shaped lead cames range from $\frac{1}{4}''$ to $1\frac{1}{2}''$ in width.

2. U-shaped came is used for edging panels and for lamp shade edges.

3. Came with an open heart is used for insertion of reinforcing rods when it is desirable to hide them.

4. Came with an off-center heart is used for outer edges to allow more trimming area in window installations.

Next wrap the lead channel, the U-shaped came, snugly around the outside edge of each piece of glass. If U-shaped came is not available, you can trim off the flanges on one side of some standard H-shaped $\frac{1}{4}''$ lead came. Using a sharp mat knife, cut the lead came so that the edges butt together, forming a joint or seam. Place the seam of each piece so that it will meet the seam of the adjacent piece when they are fastened together. Now solder the seam of each piece.

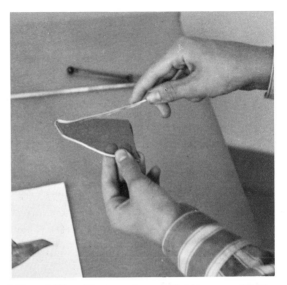

(Above) Wrap U-shaped came tightly around each glass piece, especially where it turns a sharp corner. (Below) To make an even joint, use a knife to trim the lead came where it projects beyond the last corner of the piece.

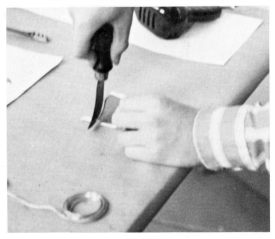

The heavy-duty soldering iron shown here can be used for almost any stained-glass project. A soldering gun is useful for spot soldering or when you are soldering only one or two joints at a time. The heat turns off automatically when the trigger is released.

Arrange the wrapped, soldered pieces to form your design. Apply solder on the front side of each piece where the seam of one piece makes contact with the seam of the adjacent piece. When all of the pieces are soldered on the front side, turn the ornament over carefully and solder at the contact points on the back. Solder a wire loop on top at the balancing point. To locate this point, catch the bottom edge of the lead with a sharp pick and hold it up. Try different spots until you find the point at which the ornament hangs straight. Use nylon fish line to hang your ornament in a window where it will catch the sunlight.

Soldering

If you have a new soldering iron, the copper tip must be tinned (solder coated) before you can use it. To do this, plug in the iron and bring it up to "hot" (5–6 minutes). Sprinkle rosin on a flat piece of copper and rub the tip of the iron into the rosin, at the same time holding the solder next to the tip. The solder will flow on, making the tip shiny. If, after repeated use, your soldering iron tip becomes rough and corroded, file it down to the copper base and repeat the procedure.

Soldering is simple if you remember these four basic rules: use clean lead, the proper solder, the right heat, and a clean soldering iron tip. Since lead oxidizes in time, it needs to be cleaned with fine steel wool prior to soldering. Lead solder is now made with a special flux core. It has a low melting point and contains just the right amount of flux to allow it to flow smoothly across the seams. Successful soldering requires that the iron tip be hot enough to melt the solder, but not so hot that it melts the lead. To heat the lead, hold the tip of the iron close to but not touching it. Touch solder to the tip of the soldering iron and apply this droplet immediately to the heated lead seam. The solder should flow smoothly into the lead seam. With practice you will learn to use the minimum amount of solder necessary.

The temperature of the soldering iron has to be watched carefully. At the correct heat, a piece of solder held against the tip will melt readily. If the iron becomes too hot it will melt the lead came; if too cool it will not melt the solder. You can test your soldering iron on scrap pieces of lead to judge the temperature.

You risk burning your fingers if you use too short a piece of solder. ⟶

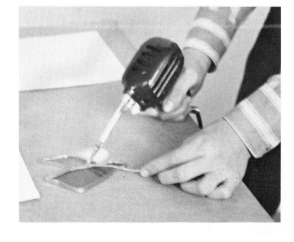

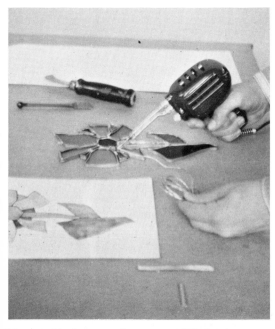

Many soldering guns have a small light that goes on when you hold the trigger, indicating that heat is flowing to the point. It generally takes seven to eight seconds for the point to heat up enough to melt solder.

As a final step, file any rough, unsightly protrusions of solder off the face of the ornament. ⟶

Stained Glass Mobile

Additional Materials Checklist:
20-gauge copper wire
24-gauge copper wire
Wire cutting shears

In constructing a mobile, you can take advantage of odd shapes of glass from the scrap box or any unusual pieces left over from other projects. A simple free-form design, suggested by the shapes of the scrap pieces themselves can be arranged without a preliminary sketch. The mobile in the illustrations was inspired by the falling leaf forms of several scrap pieces. Additional leaf shapes in autumn colors were cut to complete the arrangement. You can, of course, recut scrap pieces to improve the arrangement.

To start a mobile, make three groups of glass patterns which will balance each other in the finished mobile. Remember that a few large pieces balance many small ones. Tape each group together with transparent tape and hold the arrangement up to the light to judge the color

Cutting all the pieces of the same color at one time speeds up the job.

effect. After removing the tape, wrap each piece of glass separately in $\frac{1}{8}''$ U-shaped lead came. Butt the lead at the joint and solder.

Put the pieces of glass now enclosed in lead back down on the table in the proper arrangement. Cut pieces of 20-gauge wire to the length you have planned for between the pieces of glass. Solder the wire at the correct spot on the lead came.

You can also attach the pieces of glass to one another by first soldering small loops to the lead came and connecting them with thin wire. This allows each of the pieces of glass to move independently.

Next cut two pieces of 24-gauge copper wire for the two top supporting pieces and bend them to the proper curve. Now solder each grouping of glass pieces to the correct end of the top wires.

Suspend the different sections of the mobile and, if necessary, add or subtract pieces to improve the balance.

Mobiles or pendants are especially attractive when placed in direct sunlight so as to cast colorful shadows onto nearby surfaces. The slightest air movement turns the elements, creating constantly changing patterns of color and reflections.

When the mobile is hung you may find that the balance of the parts is not just the way you wish. One solution is to add a piece of glass to increase the weight of one grouping or remove a piece from another grouping. To finish your mobile, wipe it off with a damp cloth, then polish it with a clean dry cloth. Solder the hanging wire to the top of the first supporting rod. Hang your mobile near a light source and, as it revolves, it will reflect a constantly changing pattern of light and color onto the walls of the room.

Kinds of Stained Glass

Clear glass is basically melted sand. Color comes from different metallic compounds mixed with the molten glass before it is blown into sheets. For example, gold is used to produce beautiful rubies (hence the higher cost), cobalt and ultramarine for blues, uranium and copper for green, selenium for yellow and orange.

Stained glass varies in texture, color, thickness and degree of transparency. Some types of glass are easier to cut than others and each produces its own artistic effect.

Here are some common types of glass:

1. Antique handblown glass—usually English or European.
2. Seedy antique—blown glass with little bubbles trapped inside.
3. Cathedral glass— granite texture.
4. Opalescent glass—a varicolored translucent glass similar to the Tiffany glass used in lampshades.
5. English streaky.
6. Cathedral glass—variegated texture.
7. Blenko glass—an American handblown glass.
8. Cathedral glass—pebble texture.

1.   2.   3.   4.

5.   6.   7.   8.

15

Leaded Window Medallion

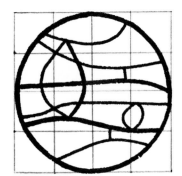

Additional Materials Checklist:
  $\frac{3}{16}''$ or $\frac{1}{4}''$ H-shaped lead came
  Metal vice
  Lead-cutting knife (a linoleum knife sharpened
    on the outside curve)
  1″ nails
  Small hammer
  White lead putty
  Putty knife
  Commercial whiting
  Scrub brushes
  Steel wool

Any window in your home can be made lovely and inviting by the introduction of a leaded glass medallion, attractive on the inside by day and colorful on the outside by night. The technique of producing leaded glass windows has varied little since medieval craftsmen created the inspired windows of the great cathedrals. We now use extruded lead cames (grooved rods) instead of casting them ourselves, an electric soldering iron rather than one heated in a fire and a steel-wheeled glass cutter instead of a hot rod of iron—other than this, the essentials of the craft remain the same.

In planning a project of this magnitude, you will want to follow the professional practice of making several preliminary designs to scale—1″ or $\frac{1}{2}''$ to 1′ is customary. Stained glass designers use

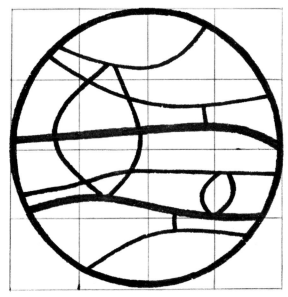

You can enlarge a small-scale drawing to actual size by "squaring off" and transferring it free-hand to a set of larger squares.

16

pen and India or Pelican ink to indicate lead lines and watercolor paints to fill in the colored glass areas as this closely approximates the final effect of the panel. First measure the pane of glass in the window that the medallion will be placed in and then, using a pencil, sketch in your design lightly to the above scale. Block in the lead lines and border with India ink and apply transparent washes of watercolor (India ink is not dissolved by watercolor). Several sketches can be made to try different effects—colors, lead widths, etc. The basic shape of the medallion can be rectangular, diamond-shaped or circular. Fruit or vegetable forms in a circular shape can be simply designed for easy leading.

The Cartoon

When you have decided on the final design, you must then enlarge the small sketch to full size (this is called a "cartoon"—the artist's traditional name for full-size detailed drawings). If your design is simple, you may be able to draw it freehand in full size following your small sketch. Most artists, however, enlarge by "squaring off." This is accomplished by dividing your sketch into squares and dividing your full-size paper into an equal number of squares. You then transfer the design from each small square to the larger square. The full-size drawing must be done with great accuracy as all dimensions of the actual glass panel are taken from it. Color selection, however, is usually made from the original color sketch.

Charcoal is an excellent medium for this full-size drawing. Lines can be easily changed and shifted when necessary, yet it is black enough

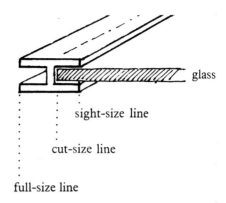

glass

sight-size line

cut-size line

full-size line

for indication of lead lines. When you are satisfied with the look of it, spray it with fixative to prevent smudging.

Three vital measurements are indicated on the drawing above:

1. Full-size line—this represents the outer edge or perimeter of the finished panel.

2. Sight-size line—this indicates the inside line of the lead came.

3. Cut-size line—this shows where the glass itself will end when inserted into the came.

Once your full-size cartoon is complete, you still need two additional full-size sheets—one for paper patterns for cutting glass, and one as a working drawing to serve as a leading guide.

Put two blank sheets on a table with the full-size cartoon on the top and pieces of carbon paper in between. Tack through the corners of all three sheets and carbons so that the papers will not shift as you trace the lines. While the sheets are still tacked down, number each individual segment that will be a cut piece of glass. Start numbering at the lower left and end with the upper right segments. Later on, when the pattern is cut apart,

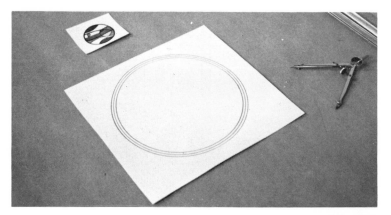

You must clearly mark the full-size, sight-size and cut-size lines of the outside lead came on the cartoon before indicating the inside lead lines.

you will keep the numbered paper pattern with the piece of cut glass so you will always know its relative position in the panel. Also write the appropriate color name on each pattern.

Separate the sheets and you are ready to cut your paper patterns from one of the copies. A professional double-bladed pattern shears is useful here but not really essential. Two single-edge razor blades taped together with a $\frac{1}{16}''$ wood or cardboard spacer in between make a good substitute (see drawing).

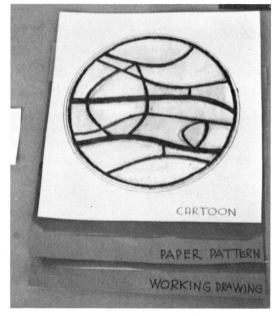

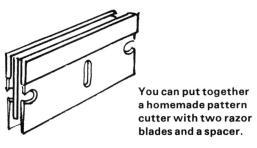

You can put together a homemade pattern cutter with two razor blades and a spacer.

Mark each of the three sheets for later identification by labelling the top paper "cartoon," the middle "paper pattern" and the bottom "working drawing."

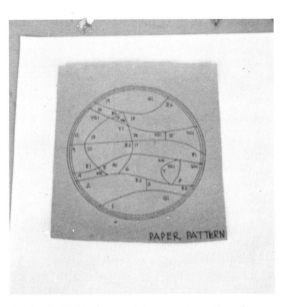

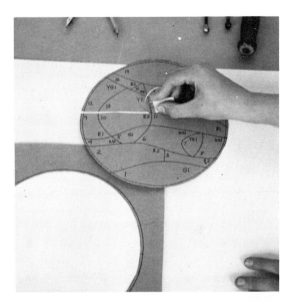

(Above) Write the position number of each segment at the left side of each paper pattern, the color name or number at the right side. (Right) First cut the long major lines which divide the panel, then the smaller subdivisions.

The two razor blades or shears cut the paper pattern to the cut-size for each piece of glass, allowing for the width of the lead heart which comes between the pieces of glass. Cut the outer perimeter cut-size line with a single blade. As you cut out the paper patterns, place them in their correct position on top of the second copy, your working drawing.

Keep the paper patterns in order as you cut them so that you will be able to place them back on the cartoon easily.

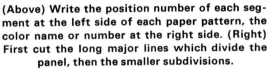

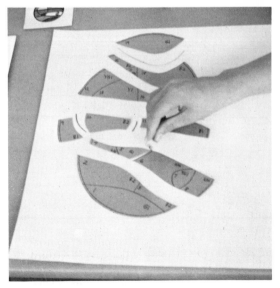

Arrange the paper patterns for the same color to take maximum advantage of the glass piece.

←

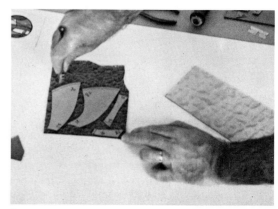

Score the more difficult curves first, then the other cuts.

CARTOON

←

Before starting to lead, check the fit of the cut segments by arranging them in position on top of the full-size cartoon.

Now cut the pieces of selected glass using the paper pattern as shown in the illustration. Glass must be cut very accurately to the paper pattern or leading will be difficult. As each pattern of glass is cut, return it to its proper place on the working drawing (with its paper pattern). When all pieces are cut, you are ready to begin leading. Take the glass segments off your working drawing and arrange them in numerical sequence next to your work bench or table. Staple or tape your working drawing to the top of your work bench.

When stretching short pieces of lead came, pull with just enough force to straighten the lead.

Run a sharpened pencil dipped in linseed oil down each groove to open the flanges of the lead came. Opening them allows different thicknesses of stained glass to fit into the came.

Before lead came is used, it must be stretched to straighten it and to take up any slack. A vice and pliers are the only tools you need. Tighten one end of the lead in a vice. Grip the other end firmly with the pliers and pull with enough pressure so that a 6' length of lead stretches 2" or 3". Leads must also be opened up by running a sharpened pencil through each groove to force the edges apart.

Run the perimeter came around the form, pressing it up against the wood. Use U-shaped came for the outside border if the medallion is to be free hanging. Use off-center H-shaped came which provides extra trimming space to install windows in specific openings.

Make a cut-out in a piece of $\frac{1}{4}''$ plywood that is the exact size and shape of the opening in which the window will be placed. If you are making a free-hanging medallion, cut the form to its finished size and shape. Nail the plywood over the working drawing. You may find it easier to cut the form in half, nailing the top part in place only after you have finished leading the bottom section of the medallion. Butt a piece of $\frac{1}{4}''$ came up against the plywood, running it completely around the perimeter. Allow the ends to overlap an inch or two when you cut it. A handy, inexpensive tool for cutting lead can be made by sharpening the reverse (bottom) side of a linoleum cutting knife. A firm, slightly rocking motion directly down on the lead is the best way to cut.

Now insert the first piece of glass into the lead grooves at the lower left. Tap the glass in slightly with the wooden handle of your knife. Now place a piece of lead along the top of the glass, fitting the glass into the groove. Add the second piece of glass and lead and continue following the numbered sequence. Where leads meet at the joints, fit the end of one into the side of the other or butt them. Put all the pieces of glass and lead down in this manner until the medallion is complete. Then bring together the open, perimeter came ends, and cut and solder where they join. Carefully tap the lead came flat at each joint with a hammer.

Soldering each of the joints comes next. Set your soldering iron to heat and, when it is hot,

Slip the point of the lead cutting knife under the ends of the lead strips and bend them up slightly so that the next piece of lead will fit into them easily. ➡️

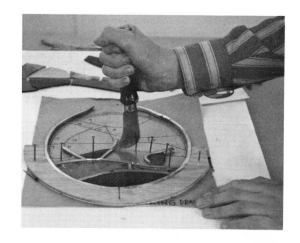

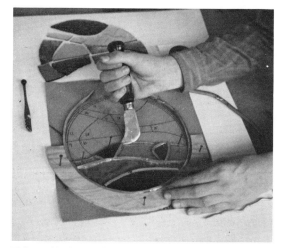

Trim off the ends of the lead strips as close to the glass as possible without actually touching the glass itself.

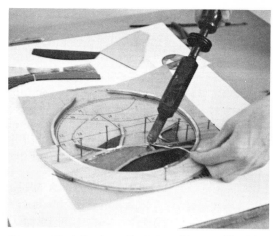

Be sure that the iron tip is touching and heating the lead as you feed solder into the joint.

touch solder and the iron tip to the joint simultaneously. The solder should flow evenly over the joint, although to do this may take a little practice. Fortunately, joints that are not soldered too smoothly have that interesting "handmade" look.

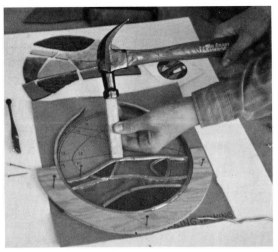

After you have leaded several pieces, tighten the panel by tapping the came with a piece of wood.

When all of the joints on one side are soldered, remove the plywood form and carefully hold the panel up to the light. At this point you can, if necessary, change a color or replace a cracked piece of glass. Put the panel down with the unsoldered side up. Pry up the lead rim around the piece to be changed. Cut a fresh piece of glass slightly smaller than the first one and put it in place. Press the lead down again and solder at the joints around this piece. When you are satisfied with the appearance of the panel, solder up all the joints on this side.

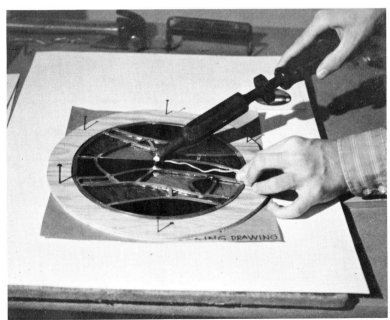

Turn the panel over and fit it once again into the form before soldering the back joints.

24

Press putty into all the openings on both sides of the panel in order to weatherproof it completely. Use a stiff-bladed putty knife to press down the face of the lead strips.

The final process before installing your medallion is to putty the panel. Lay the panel flat on your work table and, with your thumb and fingers, press white lead putty into all the lead grooves on one side of the panel to seal them. Carefully press down on all the leads with a putty knife and cut off any excess putty with a sharp piece of wood. Repeat this operation on the other side of the panel to make it fully weatherproof. Sprinkle whiting on the panel and scrub with a stiff brush to clean off any remaining putty or dirt. Finally, polish with a soft cloth.

To make a form for large rectangular panels, simply nail $\frac{1}{4}$"-thick wooden strips to a plywood base along the full-size lines. Panels that exceed about 12" × 24" need reinforcing bars across the back for support. Put $\frac{3}{8}$" wide galvanized iron bars at right angles to the panel and solder them to both edges and to each lead they cross.

Brushing commercial whiting into the panel cleans the glass and absorbs excess oil from the putty.

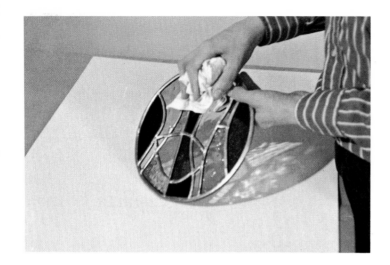

To give the lead a silvery shine, polish it with fine steel wool and then coat it with clear lacquer.

The shimmer and texture of stained glass is accentuated by the light and shade of the outside view.

Stained Glass Lighting Fixture

Additional Materials Checklist:
  Light socket, cord, and supporting chain

This project demonstrates how stained glass can be used to create attractive three-dimensional objects. A hanging lamp of stained glass fills an area with both color and light. Using the same techniques, a lamp shade, a lantern, even an unusual waste basket can be easily made.

Your design sketch in this case should be in perspective, for you to properly visualize the final effect. The basic form of the fixture illustrated is octagonal and it is best to use a dense, translucent glass which will diffuse the light of the electric bulb.

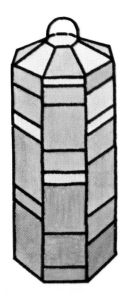

Before you start construction, use color sketches to determine which colors and shades of glass to use in order to create the effect you want. First assemble and solder the main section of the lamp flat. Then bend the soft lead easily into the finished shape. As you add each piece of glass, use the end of your knife handle to tap it into the lead grooves.

Use nails as you proceed with the leading to keep the glass and came securely in place. Since the short horizontal leads are the same length, you can cut them all beforehand to save trimming time.

The main wrap-around section of the fixture is fabricated first following the same procedure as for a flat leaded panel. Use $\frac{1}{4}''$ U-shaped lead came for all edge leading and $\frac{1}{8}''$-wide H-shaped came for the other leads.

When the main section is completely leaded and soldered, carefully stand it upright and bend the panel a little bit at a time at each vertical lead until the two edges meet, forming the octagon. Solder the joint where the two edges meet.

Using the completed main section as a guide, draw a full-size pattern for the top section. Lead this section in the same way as the main section, leaving an opening at the top for the cord to the light socket to pass through.

Use a minimum amount of solder on the joints so that the vertical leads will bend easily.

Bend the lamp body equally at each vertical lead, bringing the ends slowly together.

To hold the ends together for proper soldering, put a piece of string or a strong rubber band around the lamp body.

Now solder the top section to the main body. To finish off the edge where the two sections meet, a piece of $\frac{1}{4}''$ flat lead (which you can cut from the $\frac{1}{4}''$ came) can be soldered all round, covering any unevenness in the joints.

Finally, insert a standard light socket with cord into the lantern, allowing the cord to pass through the opening at the top. Secure the socket with solder. Attach a supporting chain to the top of the lantern by running a piece of flat lead through the bottom link of the chain and soldering the ends to the top section.

Pass a curved piece of lead through the bottom link of the hanging chain and then solder it to the top of the fixture.

If the finished fixture will be exposed to weather, putty the leads on the outside of the lamp. This is not necessary if the fixture is to hang inside the house.

Leaded Glass Piano

Three-dimensional stained-glass objects not only reflect color and light from their many different angles but also cast interesting shadow patterns.

Additional Materials Checklist:
    Striped opalescent glass
    Thin cardboard for mock-up
    $\frac{1}{8}''$ H-shaped came

Musical instruments built to scale and fabricated with stained glass make a charming home ornament. A piano with a seated pianist is a relatively easy project. Since the measurements for this project must be exact, you need to make a preliminary mock-up from heavy paper or light cardboard.

Look at an actual piano or a photograph and make a sketch simplifying each part into a flat plane. Now cut and fit paper patterns for each element in the piano. Fasten the paper patterns together with tape. Adjust or remake any parts necessary to produce a perfectly fitted, correctly proportioned model. Do the same with the figure and stool. Number each paper pattern and mark it with the color of glass to be used. The piece of striped opalescent glass will make an ideal keyboard.

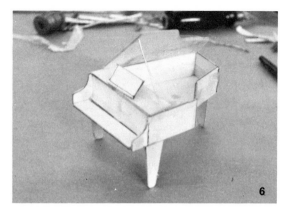

Remove the tape and accurately cut the glass pieces according to the patterns. Wrap the individual pieces in H-shaped came, soldering each joint. Next assemble the main body of the piano by soldering the top and bottom of each piece. Use tape or rubber bands to hold the model together while soldering. Use several thin pieces of wire as reinforcing rods to stabilize the legs and to support the open top. Clean and polish the model.

A piano, of course, is just one of many forms that can be reproduced in miniature. Animals, birds, boats, and antique cars are only a few of the other possibilities. Abstract, three-dimensional stained glass constructions are an exciting art form.

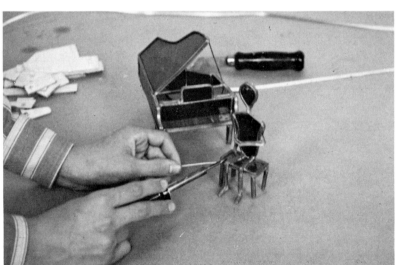

Use lead strips which can be bent easily into position for the arms and legs of the figure.

Stained Glass Lamp Shade

Additional Materials Checklist:

Opalescent glass   Toothpicks
Plastic foam (Styrofoam) form   Tracing paper
Gesso   Lamp parts and wiring

A moderate amount of experience in working with glass and ordinary equipment is all that is needed to create beautiful lamp shades in either Tiffany or contemporary style. Plastic foam lamp shade forms in a variety of sizes and shapes are available ready-made from stained glass suppliers, but the creative craftsman can make his own from plastic foam or soft wood.

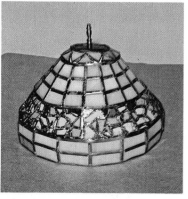

A large, neat table top is essential when you are working with the many small pieces of glass that go into a stained-glass lamp shade. A piece of old carpet tacked on the bench top provides an excellent surface for cutting glass.

Some of the most popular Tiffany type shades are:

A few contemporary type shades are:

To make your own shade form, glue layers of plastic foam (Styrofoam) together and place a weight on top of them while they dry overnight.

To make your own shade form, glue layers of plastic foam (Styrofoam) together and place a weight on top of them while they dry overnight.

Use a coping saw, a backsaw as shown here, or a hack saw blade to shape the plastic foam form.

A relatively simple shape is the best choice for your first lamp shade project. A curved form about 12″ across at the bottom and 3″ at the top is easily worked. Draw a full-size profile of the basic form on heavy paper. If a block of plastic foam thick enough for the entire form is not available, glue three or four layers together with white glue or rubber cement until the correct height of 8″ is achieved. Using the paper profile as a guide, cut the plastic foam to shape with a coping saw. Final adjustment to the exact shape is accomplished with a block of wood covered with rough sandpaper. Give the surface a final smoothing with fine sandpaper.

37

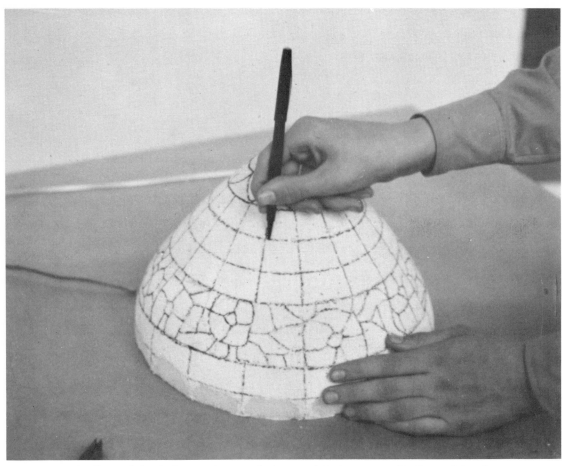

Draw in the lines of the design so they are dark enough to be seen easily through tracing paper.

Paint the outer surface of the form with two coats of white gesso. When this is dry, use charcoal to draw the lampshade design directly onto the surface of the form. The charcoal lines are easily wiped off, allowing for changes. Use a felt-tip marker to establish the final lead lines of the design. The general color scheme can be indicated by coloring between the lines with colored felt-tip markers, giving a good idea of what the completed lamp shade will look like.

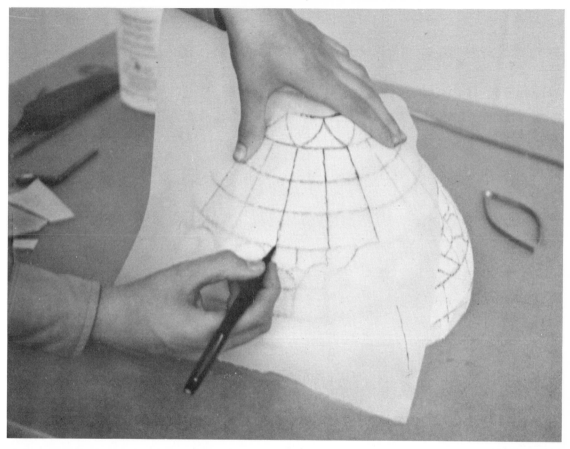

On a curved shape, trace each quarter section of the design separately to prevent distortion of the drawing.

Once the design is finalized on the plastic foam form, copy the patterns onto tracing paper, transferring this to a flat drawing which you will use as a cutting guide for the glass. Number each paper pattern and indicate your color selection.

Since the design on the form will serve as the leading guide, only the one flat drawing is needed. Use pattern shears or two razor blades taped together to cut out the paper patterns.

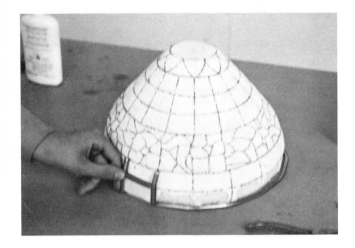

As the leading progresses, you can use toothpicks stuck into the plastic foam to hold the sections together and in place on the form.

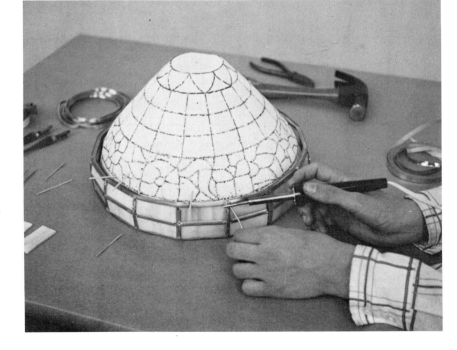

Until you have some experience with soldering, you may find it easier to solder the joints each time you add a piece of glass and lead came to the shade.

To simplify cutting and leading, use glass of uniform thickness for the small pieces of the leafy band. You can cut light-color glass directly over the pattern.

When all of the glass has been selected and cut to pattern, begin leading at the bottom of the form with a circle of U-shaped came (channel up). Butt and solder the joint of the first piece of came. Next place the first piece of glass in position. Use $\frac{3}{16}''$ H-shaped lead came as indicated by the design. Stick toothpicks into the form to hold both glass and lead in place. After leading the first row of glass pieces, solder each joint.

The backing of the copper foil is self-sticking and will hold tightly when pressed firmly around the edge of a piece of glass.

Continue leading upwards to where the leaf and flower shapes begin. For these you will use $\frac{1}{8}''$ H-shaped came instead of the $\frac{3}{16}''$-wide material as it will be easier to follow the more complex shapes with the thinner lead. Solder the joints as soon as you have leaded six or seven pieces.

The Copper Foil Method

Stained glass craftsmen use the so-called copper foil method to construct lamp shades when the design is unusually intricate. The preliminary steps up to the cutting of the paper patterns are the same. At this point, however, a single-edge razor or a mat knife must be used to cut the paper patterns since the foil does not take up any appreciable amount of space between the glass pieces.

When all the glass pieces have been cut to pattern, each edge is wrapped in adhesive-backed copper foil. The final assembly is done from the bottom of the shade upwards and each piece is held with toothpicks as with the leaded technique. Solder is applied along all of the seams and at every joint. The film of solder flows between the pieces of glass and over the surface of the copper foil. The appearance of the finished shade is the same as one made with traditional lead came.

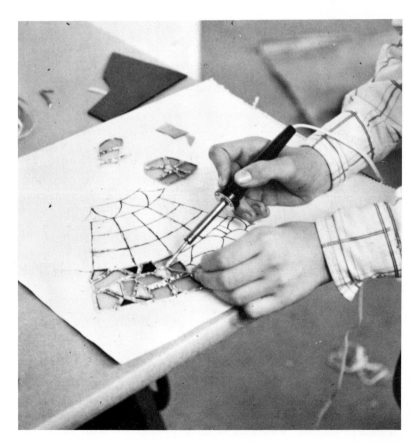

Spot solder each section of glass directly over the paper pattern spread out on a flat surface. Then place the section on the form and curve it gently into position.

Solder the sections of glass together on the form. If you use the copper foil method for the leafy band, solder the edges into the lead channel.

Lamp shades are normally made of opalescent glass which not only diffuses the light well, but is also opaque enough to hide the bulb and socket on the inside of the shade. Color selections for the shade depend upon individual taste, but analogous colors such as blue-green, blue, and blue-violet will give a harmonious glow to the shade while strong contrasting colors create a bright, lively effect. In the lampshade illustrated here, white milky glass was used for the main rectangular pieces to set off the band of brighter colors of the leaf and fruit shapes.

You can easily fill in any small openings between the pieces of glass in the leafy band with a drop or two of solder.

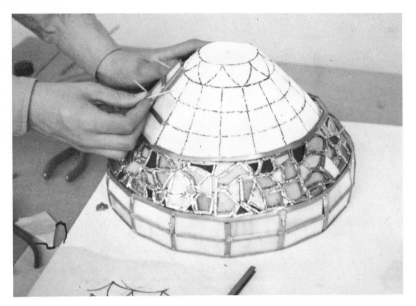

Where many lead strips are to be the same length, you may want to pre-cut them for faster assembly.

After all of the face joints are soldered, carefully remove the shade from the form and solder the inside of all the joints. For greater stability, curve heavy wire around the inside and solder it in place.

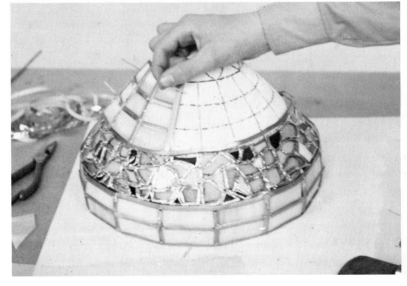

For final assembly, you need a bulb socket and fittings. These are of various types depending upon whether you are making a hanging lamp or attaching it to a base. Electrical supply shops or hardware dealers can supply the materials and show you how to connect them.

Finish off the top edge of the shade once again using U-shaped came. Finally, remove the shade from the form and solder all the joints on the inside. If necessary, heavy wire can be curved, fitted, and soldered to the inside perimeter of the shade. A hanging strap must be soldered across the top of the shade. Bore a hole in the center of the hanging strap for the lamp rod.

47

Index

Sources of Glass Supplies and Equipment

A free catalog of materials and equipment is available by mail from Whittemore-Durgin Glass Co., Box 2065 AB, Hanover, Mass. 02339.

In the United States:

Acme Glass Co.
2215 W. Roosevelt Rd.
Chicago, Ill. 60608

Art Glass of Arizona, Inc.
2047 N. 16th St.
Phoenix, Ariz. 85006

Arts & Crafts Studio
7221 Little River Turnpike
Annandale, Va. 22003

Augustine Glass Works
929 B Pico Blvd.
Santa Monica, Cal. 90405

S.A. Bendheim Co., Inc.
122 Hudson St.
New York, N.Y. 10013

Franklin Art Glass Studios
222 E. Sycamore St.
Columbus, Ohio 43206

Glass Masters Guild
621 Avenue of the Americas
New York, N.Y. 10011

Glass Work Bench
159 Main St.
Flemington, N.J. 08822

Nervo Studios
7th & Addison Streets
Berkeley, Calif. 94710

Stained Glass-Etc.
P.O. Box 106
Hathaway Pines, Calif. 95233

Stained Glass Studio
12519 Lake City Way N.E.
Seattle, Wash. 98125

Stancraft
2005 Highway 35
Oakhurst, N.J. 07755

Whittemore-Durgin Glass Co.
825 Market St.
Rockland, Mass. 02339

Willet Stained Glass Studios
10 E. Moreland Ave.
Philadelphia, Pa. 19118

In England:

Berlyne-Bailey and Company Ltd.
29 Smedley Lane
Cheetham, Manchester M8 8XB